Awesome Asian Animals

A+ books

Rhinoceroses

Are Awesome!

by Allan Morey

Consultant: Jackie Gai, DVM
Wildlife Vet

raintree
a Capstone company — publishers for children

Raintree is an imprint of Capstone Global Library Limited, a company incorporated in England and Wales
having its registered office at 7 Pilgrim Street, London, EC4V 6LB – Registered company number: 6695582

www.raintree.co.uk
myorders@raintree.co.uk

Edited by Michelle Hasselius
Designed by Peggie Carley
Picture research by Tracy Cummins
Production by Morgan Walters
Printed and bound in China.

ISBN 978-1-474-70254-6
19 18 17 16 15
10 9 8 7 6 5 4 3 2 1

British Library Cataloguing in Publication Data
A full catalogue record for this book is available from the British Library.

Acknowledgements
AP Photo: Achmad Ibrahim, 28, Kin Cheung, 27 Top; Capstone Press: 12; Dreamstime: Kmlauer, 19, Michael
Elliott, Cover Bottom; FLPA: Alain Compost/Biosphoto, 13, Terry Whittaker, 15; Getty Images: Reto Puppetti, 5;
iStockphoto: jezphotos, 27 Bottom, Matt Naylor, 18 Bottom; Minden Pictures: Suzi Eszterhas, 20, 21, ZSSD, 23,
26, 29 Left; Newscom: Suzi Eszterhas/Minden Pictures, 9; Shutterstock: Alan Jeffery, 22, Christian Musat, 17 Top,
Eric Isselee, Cover Back, Cover Top, Cover Middle, 1, 6 Bottom, 30, 32 Bottom, Ewan Chesser, 6 Top, ilovezion,
7, JeremyRichards, 29 Right, Jonathan Tichon, 18 Top, kongsak sumano, 25, neelsky, 4, 16, 24, PeterVrabel, 8,
Rigamondis, Design Element; Thinkstock: Anup Shah, 11; Wikimedia: Ltshears, 10, 14, 17 Bottom

We would like to thank Jackie Gai, DVM, for her invaluable help in the preparation of this book.

Contents

Amazing rhinoceroses

Ba-boom! Ba-boom! The earth shakes. Heavy footsteps thud on the ground. A large animal bursts through the trees. Is it a tank with horns? No, it's a rhinoceros!

Rhinos are one of the world's largest land animals. But that is just one reason this animal is so amazing.

Tanks with horns

An adult rhinoceros has a horn at the top of its nose. Rhinoceros actually means "nose horn". Some rhinos also have a small horn on their foreheads.

Rhino horns are similar to a horse's hooves
or a turtle's beak. They are all made out of
the same tough material, called keratin.

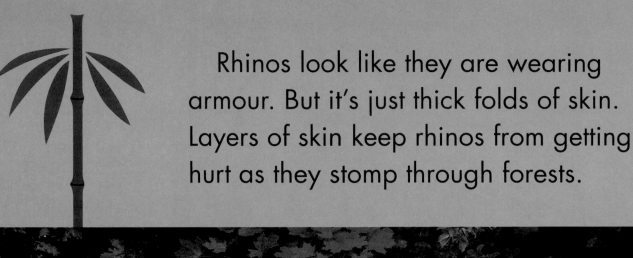

Rhinos look like they are wearing armour. But it's just thick folds of skin. Layers of skin keep rhinos from getting hurt as they stomp through forests.

Rhinos roll around in mud like pigs on a farm. Mud protects their skin from the sun and insect bites.

Rhinos are big. They can weigh up to around 3 tons, depending on the type of rhinoceros. That's as much as some cars weigh! Rhinos can measure more than 1.8 metres (6 feet) tall at the shoulders.

Rhinos cannot see well. But rhinos hear even the smallest sounds with their cup-shaped ears. Rhinos use their excellent sense of smell to find food.

Three of a kind

Three types of rhinoceroses live in Asia. The Javan rhino is found only in Ujung Kulon National Park in Java, Indonesia. Less than 50 Javan rhinos live in the park. Javan rhinos are one of the rarest animals in the world.

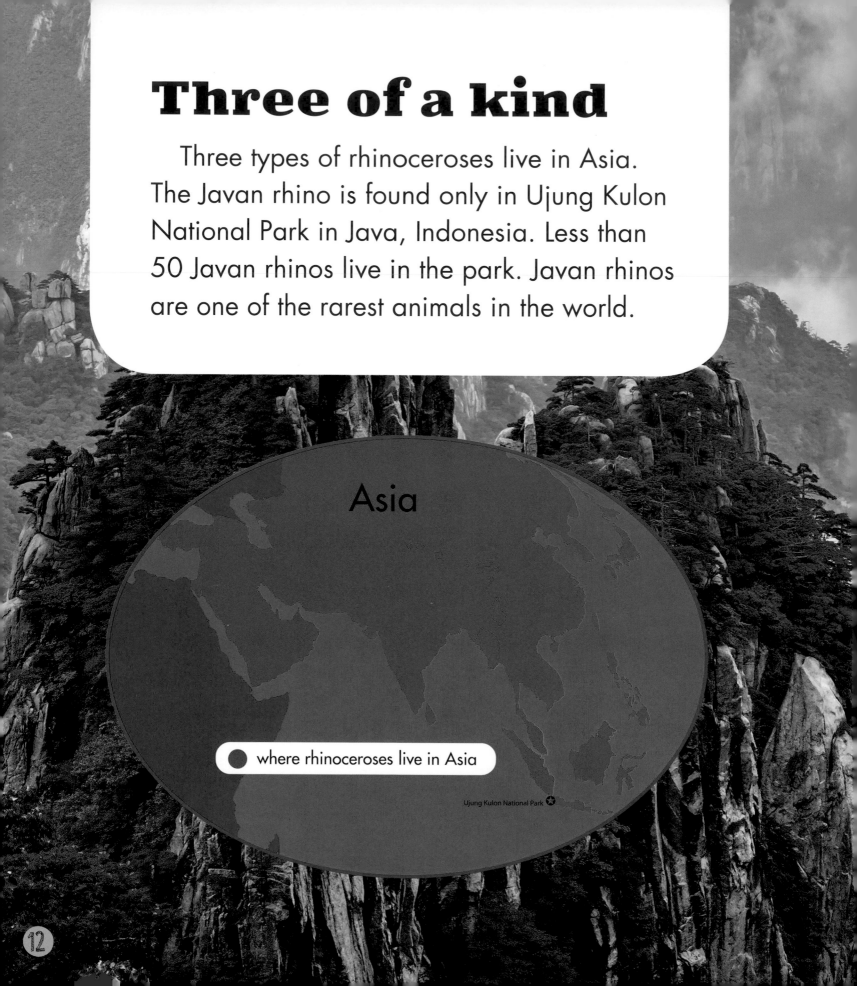

Asia

● where rhinoceroses live in Asia

Ujung Kulon National Park ✪

Javan rhino

The Sumatran rhino is sometimes called
the hairy rhino. Unlike other rhinos, Sumatran
rhinos are covered with dark hair.

Most Sumatran rhinos live in Indonesia. They roam through the country's forests and swamps. They can also be found in the mountain forests of Malaysia.

Indian rhinoceroses live mostly in north-east India. Rivers often flood in this area. It's a good thing Indian rhinos can swim. They dive under water in search of food. Indian rhinos also live in the forests and grasslands of southern Nepal. Sometimes Indian rhinoceroses are called greater one-horned rhinoceroses.

Chomp! Chomp! Rhinos are herbivores. They eat plants that grow near their homes. But rhinos aren't fussy. They graze on grasses. They eat fallen fruit and chew on tree leaves. If they live near rivers, they also eat plants that grow in the water.

Bulls, cows and calves

Male rhinos are called bulls. Females are called cows. Bulls and cows spend most of their time apart. But they come together to mate.

A pregnant female gives birth to a calf after 15 to 16 months. Cows will have one calf every few years.

rhino calf

Calves can weigh more than 45 kilograms
(100 pounds) when they are born. Calves
stay with their mothers for two or three years.

Too big to eat

Adult rhinos do not have predators in the wild. They are too big. And, rhinos have deadly horns, sharp teeth and tough skin. Most other animals leave them alone. But a hungry tiger might kill a young or sick rhino. A healthy rhino can live for up to 40 years in the wild.

Humans are the biggest danger to
rhinoceroses. Rhinos once lived throughout
much of Africa and Asia. Now all three Asian
rhinos are in danger of becoming extinct.

People have killed thousands of rhinos for their horns. People use the horns to make medicines and jewellery.

Saving the rhinos

Today, wildlife groups raise money to help save rhinos. Governments have made it against the law to hunt rhinos.

Together they have set up wildlife parks. Rhinos can safely live in these areas, and their numbers are growing.

Glossary

armour protective covering

extinct no longer living; an extinct animal is one that has died out, with no more of its kind

graze eat grass and other plants

herbivore animal that eats only plants

keratin hard substance that forms a rhinoceros' horns, a turtle's beak and a horse's hooves

mate join together to produce young

medicine substance used to treat illnesses

predator animal that hunts other animals for food

territory area of land that an animal claims as its own to live in

Books

Animals in Danger in Asia, Richard and Louise Spilsbury (Raintree, 2013)

First Animal Encyclopedia, Anita Ganeri (Bloomsbury Childrens, 2013)

Introducing Asia (Introducing Continents) Anita Ganeri (Raintree, 2014)

Websites

www.bbc.co.uk/nature/life/Rhinoceros
Learn all about rhinoceroses.

http://gowild.wwf.org.uk/asia
Find out fun facts about rhinos, read stories and play games!

www.savetherhino.org/rhino_info/for_kids
Make your own rhino model and other fun crafts!

Comprehension questions

1. Turn to page 9. What is happening in this picture? Why do you think rhinos do this?

2. Rhinoceroses are herbivores. What is a herbivore?

3. Rhinos have few predators in the wild. Give two reasons why.

Index